THE GOLDEN UNDERGROUND

AFRICAN AMERICAN LIFE SERIES

A complete listing of the books in this series can be found online at wsupress.wayne.edu

Series Editors
Melba Joyce Boyd
  Department of Africana Studies, Wayne State University
Ronald Brown
  Department of Political Science, Wayne State University

THE GOLDEN UNDERGROUND

POEMS BY ANTHONY BUTTS

W | Wayne State University Press ▪ *Detroit*

13   12   11   10   09   5   4   3   2   1

Library of Congress Cataloging-in-Publication Data

Butts, Anthony.
The golden underground : poems / by Anthony Butts.
p. cm. — (African American life series)
ISBN 978-0-8143-3389-1 (pbk. : alk. paper)
I. Title. II. Series.
PS3552.U8897G65 2009
811'.54—dc22
                                              2008046704

∞

Designed by Charlie Sharp
Typeset by Maya Rhodes
Composed in Minion Pro

For the Heartbeat of God

Contents

The
Saint Brigid
Psalms

Before Autumn

Late September, on the eve of autumn, the leaves of trees
are like sirens canting, anxious for the blow which precedes
Indian summer—relieving them of husks, unlike the crinkling
of machines in the industrial village next door, air conditioners
huffing through their final ode to summer. Technology
is no stand-in for this: smoke before the screen

phosphorescent in a darkened study, an entire shelf dedicated
to King Lear—who never recovered in time—bearing his own
corpse until the end, the stultifying frailty of human nature.

The Goddess of Lake Michigan stands starkly over the horizon,
content with the future, mechanism of sleet and wind:
the logic of womanhood, that place of surprise and anxiety.

Sky parrots brilliance from below, the sun perilously lost,
light from houses—like dusk multiplying—toward
fatally high integers across the land, their glow like dust
before the human heart, protostars heating up to incandesce
for as long as necessary. Interlocutor. Inquisitor. A mind
of two halves, the heart interspersed throughout the body

like a wandering mouth, He covers this land with the sheath
of his body. He covets colors severely, seemingly no one
to blame for his indiscretion. Where lies that bridge from "here"

to "there"—that place where the two halves meet peaceably?
I don't want to know the great Sky God any more than through
his standard swelling along the horizon, his standard bearer

standing somewhere meekly I'm sure. Though I'll never know
from asking, these unbelievable characters appear cunning and—
as yet—indiscernible. I simply wander through this wilderness
set out for me, just speak to me! Though I command no army
clouds march across the sky like militant women. The seas
roil in all their discomfort, for winter, as if only for me.

Song of Starry-Eyed Children

How shade turns to light as the sun
passes through clouds, an inversion
of efforts first unearthed. Dark-haired
and in a tower above campus like Cordelia
captured by her own beliefs, a student tests
the limits of human closeness through
self-imposed isolation. Poems do not always
concern themselves with loss, though her hair
dangles truly dark. Not the student or the heroine
but the Lady of the Lake who wants

to roam in playful circles upon the waves.

Clouds curdle and coalesce in September
more than any conveyed through serif
or oil, their effort like tumultuous nature
pressing out versions of belief in every
new rendering of what we feel lying
beneath surfaces but cannot reach.
Leave the student in that tower long enough
for discord to set in, long enough to set
silence to rages imaginable, the inverse noise
in the night's quiet hours like radiation

from Three Mile Island seeping through.

Like Angelo in third grade, complacent
one moment and psychotic the next,
knowledge lies as a quilt over pressed
linen: a puffy invalid lounging. Dizzy Lear
seeks his center as if to say "dear psyche,
why hast thou forsaken me?" Sunrise;
sunset; day-flight; starkness. And wandering
will provide no cure, except for the king of France.
Deus ex machina in the form of drama masks,
ecstatic and tormented, police in their sunglasses

instead of criminals—in the end—escaping.

Or the Lady of the Lake descending and ascending,
gods must exist side-by-side with the Deity
in late hours: her influence the light
glowing orange over Kalamazoo—even if
no one else sees it. She resembles the starry-eyed
child I never noticed until I saw it in myself. Not
the darkest one I know, but someone other
in my mirror beaming back—that shell cast away,
the body like a larva sleek and capable. I am
the student and Cordelia, even Angelo, before

the Goddess of Numbers multiplying into dawn's light.

Intercession to Saint Brigid

Young and black a woman rocks back and forth
on the Greyhound to Dallas, a fulcrum of night
in her white T-shirt. A white woman farther back

dressed in black scratches the top of her head with one
fingernail like a record skipping over some song
she'd love to remember, some ode she seems

to never give up on. White crosses grow larger
in their trinities the farther we descend toward
the equator, southern culture like those high-

powered lights turned at dizzying angles upward,
faith illuminated in an attempt at the largest
manuscripts ever read. Saint Brigid is back

on Lake Michigan, the Book of Kells in my lap,
the lamplight above my head faintly culling
stronger strands from weaker ones as no one

pays attention to me or my Red Wings jersey
in the obscurity of that near-coffin rolling,
its tubular presence like the shape of a life—

that form the only person at a party who's
interesting. I will not let go of that raft.
Islands of light. Eyes of night. Fist-sized

towns pass incredulously by. Sometimes a person
pointing aimlessly on the corner resembles a pattern
interwoven in daylight, a labyrinth of sound and sight—

runes of our fate known to someone except for ourselves:
the Lady of the Lake, her hair as dark as the two
women on board. One has scratched a small

hole in her head, blood collecting in the tiny U
in her psyche. The other sits with her small girl
mewling to a music only her mother could know.

And I am all fretwork, or so I believe, in this moment
where the next buses will connect with the terra-cotta
mountains of Utah and the windswept plains of Nebraska—

upon the blackout of intercessions as darkness closes
ranks at 1:16 A.M., about an hour before Dallas where
we'll wake into the only light we'll witness on this night.

Mist and Fog

Saucers and their cousins sit respectfully in silence,
the room austere in black and white distressed checks
lining the Formica like footprints to nowhere: two rooms
separated by more than just dusky effervescence, Saint Brigid

come ashore in the form of mist and fog. Outside, no word
exists for "demure" or "dapper" as gray inhabits both places
of the mind—the last rays persevering beneath Sky's observation,
the Lady of the Lake observing a whistle's billowing

with her ears. We rely upon odd senses when in need,
the couple muttering each one to themselves as if
those cluttered rooms were populated by thoughts,
as if throw pillows were like faces passing in the reflection

of department store windows—each shopping
for their own anniversary gift, which no one thought
to give. Squirrels gather the world into their own
constituency of promise and fortitude as if no other

were available, contemplative winter a sustaining
memory of more than luck and loss. Vibration
of missing sound after rhythmic chanting mimics
the course of human history turned around:

a congregation in the loss of languages spoken
and unspoken after group meditation, after the hum
of Saint Brigid has inspired even the leaves to sing
along. Sound can only hurt you if you let it,

the couple somnambulistic in the kitchen
organizing saucers according to their own
phenomenology, the eerie mist above
dishes like miniature gymnasts

twisting in the rhythm of sentences turning:
words bending thoughts like light refracted—
the couple making love with their gestures,
even if mist is not yet in their eyes.

Song of Earth and Sky

The sun rises in its happenstance of the day,
garbage trucks like predawn crickets, the lack
of streetwalkers as its own object of desire,

life more like art than the reality we reconstruct
through daily ritual imitated. Routine is candy
for the psyche, blocks of caramel on a park bench

like children sitting calmly, a jar of chocolates
individually wrapped on His table at home
in the only version of heaven I must know.

Uncle Vanya on stage, young actors allowing
their own characters to slip through at unwarranted
intervals, the black and white of the play like

a photograph developing in liquid depths
of hydroquinone, the dark room indistinguishable
from the substance, Doctor Astrov imperceptible

to his own logic. The child's play makes them great,
that reservoir of happenstance called upon in
rough-hewn hours of practice and malcontent

like great swatches of Heaven in the form of
inspiration when blue stands out as the only color
assigned to the soul of an artist looking

skyward, when platinum orange represents
the color of subsistence before the morning star
as the great Sky God leans in for

a peek at the day and what we might bring.
He is as hokey as all that, no other
emotion as pure, as metallic as ice

in the way that it looks to others, that sentiment
seeming more like the pocket miracle of
a plastic lighter, transparent and purple

before the tip of the cigarette which might
not serve as inspiration but more like a
partner with whom the would-be Astrov

might dialogue, as if its white dress hung like
would-be wedding attire, as if Sonya would
wait forever for her man to come around.

Sky knows more than Earth will tell it,
our own fates here just as easily unwrapped
and tasted like the most forbidden of sweets,

the choicest of produce in the marketplace of our
longing, perseverance from "here" to "there"
like the last sentimental cricket inching home.

The Landscape for Growth

for Annie and Rosie

A cardboard sunflower suspended from a tree,
birdseed pasted in sprinkle pattern on that

star-shaped yellow, art keeps us moving forward:
that slant of light at nine A.M. in October

like midnight of the mind, the darkened
light ecstatic on its journey across

trees and red brick chimneys lined with ivy.
Two girls play in the backyard playground

as if the green world would remain, marigolds
gone brittle, the plastic heads of wicker witches

chasing down shadows as Sky watches
harmlessly, as Day lies like Tupperware

over the wet grassiness of morning. Evergreen,
in the absence of sunlight, will rule December,

whisper through January until the next months
seem delayed, until the only words we think

we hear become exit wounds, our ears like savages
tamed. What will the next house made of papier-

mâché mean when rain falls like cold missiles
from God—when loss becomes the landscape

for growth? The memory of green seems fierce
amidst the stark tableau of winter, the children

reminiscing about being three and at the nursery
in a way that most of us cannot. Sky watches

over as if memory prompted an assertion to remember
more, gray upon gray as the world forgets itself,

always the loss of anything but the next blizzard
piling snow over the black wrought-iron legs

of park benches, over what we choose
to forget. The two girls make patterns

in the papier-mâché as if snow already
surrounded us, the glitter of Christmas like silver

appliqué on the sweater that one would wear
to Church, about which the other will just smile

as if her expression provided an anecdote for earthy
days beneath the cold objectivity of autumn sun.

Eight Modes toward Desire

I

Downriver dining tray piled with squirrel
from someone's excursion into backyard
sports or the actual bounty of small game

hunters, its skin a syrupy sweet from a life
of digesting nuts, not all trophies are for
keeps. The planet Saturn looms like

a children's pool toy in the amateur
telescope purchased for a month's
worth of child wages, the boy having trotted

out the black-and-white tube amounting
to more than Galileo could muster
in 1610: year toward censure. Its rings

push like arms against the night
as if the circular field of view
were more like a silent movie

where the oculus of view, reduced
by the lens, collapses upon the
minnowed form of an actress-

turned-flapper, overly poignant
in her distress. The color seems
an addition as soft hues swirl

around the bend, into starlight
dotting the periphery, into the first
notion of memory he will have.

Venison will possess the taste of this night's
sugar. Water will seem like wine as
if Saturn were floating face up in the cup.

II

Sun shines like the only basis for desire,
a couple kissing in Clark Park as if their
parents were farther than the Ambassador

Bridge, the Straits of Detroit a fugue of blue,
red-hulled oil tankers headed for ports as far
as Chicago, inland seas like the world turned

inside out, an inner world made real beneath
failing autumn light. A university astronomer
makes a routine study of the sun, her students

quite mobile—their bodies like thoughts offered
before the conveying of knowledge, perfect mirrors
before the lens through which they study. Or maybe

the world does not bear this much light. Men wander the streets
looking for spare change and the upturned butts of those
who hadn't time to finish before the next appointment:

the spiral rings of their day-planners like rings of Saturn
undone. The lovers will graduate in time. Winter will push
on beneath the knowledge of Sky as we push snow to the sides

of roads and the sidewalks of our families and the elderly.
Spots in the telescope, empty bottles in the snow, lovers
who will break up before the long pull of winter has seen

them through to Valentine's Day: loss represents the truer face
of freedom, seemingly more lively than the visage of Sky.
Peer down at a galaxy of delight and sorrow, the snow more like

splotches upon the land, bottles as the accumulation of more
than just waste, the sun revealing a spectacle burrowing deep
beneath its surface: sunspots as lovers lying for the last time.

III

The somber moon waxes within its field of lament
before the harvest, the closest feeling to leaving
this Earth for some other place. I stood and watched

that unknown creature come and visit me in the night.
The air: a chilled martini. The ground: a wet napkin.
We should ignore metaphors in times like these,

the moon trapped in the northern hemisphere as if
Earth owned it, orange mortgage through the mist
of October as if moisture paid us back

for a pleasant summer. Twentieth-century castles
stand along Fifth Avenue with traffic swimming
past, the absence of simile like the nothing

inside of me when a streetwalker says
"hello." The night chills me, not really
afraid of whatever the absence of light

might bring. People gather for Taizé
in the Cathedral of Hope, the streetwalker
among them. I do not feel guilt as we chant

in unison. I feel Sky outside as if God stood
right here with us. The moon has not left
me wondering about the harvest or Halloween,

or wishing for a more telescopic vision.
The moon gathers steam from the night sky
as if the charge toward winter seemed more like

battlefield maneuvers than happenstance. The man
gathers his breath to form the one perfect word
he knows, the next one, which leaves me with peace.

IV

Flat plastic floats by on Halloween, victors
and villains poorly sheltering children from
northern drizzle. Pellets against the scent

of vinyl abrupt as the representation of black
and orange: celebrations in the basements
of two-family flats where the owner's space

becomes a shared place for the block's revelers.
His putting-green lawn gets trampled on this
one day of the year, the harvest moon like some

interloper or cosmopolitan newsman making
reports on the goings-on of the evening. Stars
shake at the news, twittering in the chill

of the last official day of autumn. Tomorrow
will bring different holidays, All Saints'
Day clothed in the gray of November like

an imposter throwing off his troubled
clothes to become the person he really should—
the first official snow falling between now

and Thanksgiving as if we give thanks
for work and not rest. The moon will
transform itself into that blue cheese

simile we've become so familiar with, though
astronomers will not detect anything alarming.
All Souls' Day will come cloaked in its only

suitable attire, garments stripped-down
of desire and yearning, the electric scent
in parishes passing on through ordinary time.

V

M31, the galaxy Andromeda visible in the northern
sky as it also appeared in the textbook I checked out
from the adult section at age ten, the stern blue

cover of the forlorn text seemingly the tenor of poetry,
its lonely calculations more than just approximations
from "here" to "there," the actual galaxy as invisible

to my eyes as the spine of the Milky Way on the savanna
somewhere in Africa. The arms of Andromeda were more
powerful than the rings of Saturn, not needing to push

against the edge of the photograph like a prisoner, its two
globular companions larger than any satellite could appear
next to Saturn. That god was even more lonely,

his children having deserted him with the other Titans,
their palms like a hundred hands of fate swooping over
the door to Tartarus. Not meant to present reality,

photographs like deities on the page, they have
misguided aims, each image overthrown by
the next scientist who will lay a claim on history.

Winter passes in such a way, snow covering over
footprints previously discovered so that other
inroads seem revolutionary. Each blizzard a gift,

a rediscovery of what Sky has left us this time,
my arms make angels in the snow when real
art hovers 2.9 million light years away, when the arms

of Andromeda spread out to welcome
its neighbors as if one might jump across the page,
as if my wings might just as easily carry me there.

VI

Manhole covers billow steam into a Detroit
winter, bodies passing in their semblance of gray
before the blizzard of '77. Uncovered, they would

make poor versions of black holes in textbooks:
the only victims, the odd inattentive person dropping
in instead of whole systems of planets and stars

gobbled down, I don't know where all this came from,
snow funneling off my blade toward ever higher banks
along the sides of my father's parking spot—his blue

Electra 225 seemingly snow plow enough to make its
way down the street at 5:45 P.M. against the flow of traffic
heading back to the suburb which housed Warren Stamping

instead of back to the city which names us Detroiters.
Collapsars, only visible through the destruction
they leave, burn a peripheral center into the page:

a donut hole darker than its star-filled plate number
4.5B in the chapter on stellar decay. Every home dies
eventually, to some, whether the passing on

of grandparents, or the passing of a star into
the red giant phase as it swallows up its children
just as Betelgeuse must have done. Shoveling

snow in winter brings about such reckonings,
that photographic plate, the warmest image
in my mind as my father segued off of I-94

onto Scotten Street, the men and women of Clark Street
Cadillac making their way in the opposite direction down
past our house like stars rushing toward destruction.

VII

If rainbows shine like salvation, what of a double spectrum
broadcasting its joy across the hemisphere above? Clouds
loomed dark on the Sabbath, as if seven represented

an unlucky number. Rain poured as the sun shined and,
as we've heard, Satan must've battered his wife again. But
on the Sabbath? We find times for literal language and times

for more literary speech, the box that restrains us gone,
the gentle mask of gray thrown over the day like the Horsehead
Nebula offering its darkened solace within a spectral

cloud—color, in its absence, bringing about such
a heavenly body as astrologers could not have predicted,
as early astronomers could not have accounted for. The

Slip and Slide glides other children past its yellow surface
as I read about the elemental desire of the universe
laid out on paper, the cover of the book black and

laminated in the way of tomes from the adult
section: resistant to coffee stains or the stray
splash of water from the others—here or in

the heavens. The Goddess of Numbers had
to be a woman, the Lady of the Lake presiding
over the bridge from "here" to "there," modes

of desire like a parked Monte Carlo shining—as
my father said—like new money, its black finish
lacquered as well as the Slip and Slide seemed to me.

Cirrus dots the sky like an abacus, their puffy
clouds taking an accounting of the earth below:
or so it seems, from the woman of my dreams.

VIII

God is not an anvil upon which the universe
is forged and reformed. A horseshoe is just
that unless we believe that its U culls more

than simple delight at the symmetry of our own
creation. We will make and remake the world
until every electron might sing instead of shimmer

in their cloud about an atom—each raindrop like
a miniature cosmos or a simple community
of Mennonites on their farms, just back from

the Greyhound connecting Ohio to Pennsylvania,
dressed in a black more matte than the most
budget-conscious black-and-white photographs

in a text on the origins of the known universe.
Community provides the box that contains us, our
colors like the universe sprawling across the tableau

of night. For each microscopic object in the sky,
the polestar aiming us steadily toward true north,
an unseen world becomes visible in the pages

of speculative texts, illuminated like the Book
of Kells presented as our next attempt at a gift
to mankind. Of black and white: the basic

images I see before me on my trek back to
Pittsburgh, Pennsylvania. Mennonite men and
women dress in their sharpest intent, native

Africans berry-black in their white and periwinkle—
the world reducible to grays if only we let it,
the journey developing right before our eyes.

Thin Places

White stick with red tip tapping the sidewalk
at casual intervals, this blind man knows his
way around: the strict passing of each stride
like a mathematics toward desire, calm world of

zeroes invisible to seemingly everyone but me—
the pace with which I lift and smoke a drag
on my cigarette just as orderly, just as rare,
as the trained smoke from my mouth seems

to others. This world is not as small as it
appears, our hands unimaginably linked
in their dance around the unknowingly
sighted world. It never mattered where

the buildings on campus lie, yellow bricks
like sunlight captured as a solid. The world
of distances the only one worth knowing,
his sleep languishes as if the next step

would not remain alone, as if the map of the earth
could have never appeared flat. We seek the thin
places of commitment, the extraordinary vision
of a world where earth and sky meet, where

the great Sky God paces about in solace. What
connections do we have with each other,
those places where earth and sky are pressed
out of existence into an awaiting horizon

of pink and powder blue at the steady lapping
of water on the shore? She lingers there,
I believe, awaiting the "yes" that trained men
possess—a woman in periwinkle and white

as if her cloak contained the approaching dawn after
the first hues have faded from clouds. The morning
appears that bright, without sunlight, in the first moments
we believe might reveal the dawn. He walks with a

cane loosely in His hand. He walks as would
a man who knows where to go; I ask
for the same, for autumn leaves to glow
like the very sun reflecting, as if they could

grow their own light. I have walked as a blind
man in the world of light conversation, as an
angel whose wings retracted permanently
into the coffered ceiling of sky. I am not immortal;

I am the only light I know before the block and tackle
hoisting of the sun, the passing of day like the building
of a community of belief—dew on lawns like songs
of lament and longing. The blind man passes

like a promise through somber morning, moisture
upon moisture until the ground seems saturated with
pleas, as if the only words I try to give resemble the ones
that would make her gown completely white.

Ice Palaces

We speak of "falling in love," as though
love were something like water that collects
in pools, lakes, rivers, and oceans. You
can "fall into" it or walk around it.
FR. THOMAS MERTON

The season is far spent, His wind billowing
white curtains as if this provided the only bliss
we could expect. Pedestrians tread upon rainbows

as leaves fall from their appointed trees,
the nothingness vivid around us. Brown,
and in those limbs, forlorn skins hang on

beneath the gray of late October: the last
oozings from leaves my only solace.
Where could I go from here, except

the stern stability of winter—first among
seasons in its meditative state of evergreen
and white. Great Sky turns gray in times

like these, the firmament of winter as the
clarion call to single men and women
that Christmas wasn't only meant for

families, the perceived lack of seasons
secreted past on the whispers of conifers.
God confesses much during long silences,

an economy of more than couples—
commandeered season of Christmas lights
and tulip bulbs awaiting the new season.

Both shine as the promise of a love that
endures, morning dew on snow as a surface
which could support bodies if needed,

the crusting of drifts like the age-old promise
that better days lie ahead, that the only
commitment which matters shall never pass.

Pygmalion

The Memory of Light

How good it is and how pleasant
for people to dwell together.
Good and pleasant, people
together.

PSALM 131:1

Smoking outside the hospital a younger
woman confesses an affair to an older one
whose first cigarette is spent with its red

tip upturned in the sand bin, gin
still fresh on her breath, a faithful
husband still recovering from arterial

sclerosis. Old news. A young man asks for
a light: "the light," he says in broken English
or so she thinks. He's been watching

the icing on her lips, thinking something
familiar, like ice on the tips of awnings
in February, when the sun sporadically

makes its appearance through layers
of gray, through the memory of light.
He has wanted this throughout the day

of his life, a Betamax moment since 1979
when the world seemed obsessed with music,
women in their kamikaze fashions

at his awakening, their woolen skirts green
steel, black walking shoes like cartoon foot-
prints made visible in the day's dried newsprint.

Soldiers

Take my yoke upon you and learn from me;
for I am gentle and humble of heart, and you
will find rest for your souls. For my yoke is easy
and my burden is light.

MATTHEW 11:29–30

A tall black man sings his way down
West Warren Avenue, spreading Motown
throughout Dearborn, the Camelot Theatre's

yellowed marquee proclaiming a sci-fi flick
as if still open for business—a nineteen-fifties donut
shop still serving the same baby boomers

who frequented this place.
Songs provide memories uncontrolled, unprescribed,
pastries going down like soldiers, the man

in his Goodwill fatigues belting off-key
like the man sitting next to me at Taizé,
his voice settling into bass against a bastion

of tenors and sopranos. We would become
soldiers in the army of God to the boy
who spoke his prayer to the masses,

rhetorical devices shuttering in the sun
like cameras flashing for the hero of the day—
the clicking of buttons a language of lament,

our harmony hallowed each time we sing
in God alone my soul can find rest and peace as if
glory had come and gone before we arrived.

Fretwork

Holy, holy, holy. My heart, my heart
adores you! My heart knows how to say
to you: Holy are you, Lord!

PSALM 116

Triangular faces, drawn in green ink, adorn
the side panels of pickup trucks from Pyramid
Auto Body Shop: bearded Chaldeans, their gold

rings and blue diamonds attesting to the wealth
of their respective families on hands dangling
over the sides of door panels as they drive

to the next stuck Buick during the latest blizzard
in Dearborn. Their language feels like the coconut
milk of Thai immigrants, with their restaurants

accumulating in this hotbed of Arabic culture.
A wanderer takes it all in, wearing the grayed
scarf a former lover gifted before kicking

him out of her house, no need for a job, as the streets—
at least—provide a similar welcome for victims
and victimizers alike, the same as in the Tudor

homes on Oakman Boulevard and West Warren Avenue.
I want to hear all their voices at once, as if the world's
languages could produce harmonious sounds, my own

Tower of Babel where I would finally find
the language to woo the woman of my dreaming,
her mythological voice an echo of God.

Voices' End

They must go through the Valley
of Thorns, but they find it
a place of springs.

PSALM 84

Notes dot the page in ways for which we
cannot account, the rise and fall of dactyls
like the rise and fall of crimson in autumn,

the stems of notes pointing our way first up
then down the scale—the wellspring of my
singing bringing a woman deaf from birth

nearby, her hearing aid angled as if to say
you too are doing well. We sing all alone
in the silence of disbelief, as if no story

had been written just for us, the voices now gone
in the clarion call of winter: its white haze
the white paper on which crows seem like

notes, its evergreen prickly as the heat
of constant thinking. Let go of every
thing, the past as holly berries on shrubs,

the future as longing in the gray and white
clouds, the present as the thin places whose
sound we must take note of. What has this

world left us but horizontal lines upon the page,
languages in verse and note, our ears tuned to
the frequency of longing, of snow flakes falling?

Embers

Little children, let us love, not in word or speech,
but in truth and action. And by this we will know
that we are from the truth and will reassure our hearts
before him whenever our hearts condemn us.

JOHN 3:17–20

Chasms hidden between words, volumes
resounding, the only presence steadfast as
midnight leaves, present as the hours of

the day—a man's body beneath a streetlamp
as the photo negative of despair: the stain
on the camera, not like God's insight. He burns

off embers of his life as his cigarette slowly
extinguishes itself, his gray flannel suit
a hypocrisy of fashion as he stands in front

of Mount Carmel Hospital waiting for the
test results of a friend at twelve in the evening:
as his life is not as straightlaced as it seems.

He could look at me forever, sorry
to say, because even in times like these
I may appear attractive. I have

a sadness which breaks as God's light across
a bay, the only space left to us the one which
we keep—that loss the only light from the ember

of a cigarette in His presence, leaves crinkling
in the easy breeze, within the loose shadows
ringing the perimeter of the parking lot.

Far from Home

I love you Lord, my strength,
My rock, my fortress, my savior.
God, you are the rock where I take refuge;
My shield, my mighty help, my stronghold.

PSALM 18

A black woman holds two seats on the bus
as if they represented the only things she owns,
the other passengers too busy to raise

a fuss, the afternoon driver alone with his own
thoughts of the day. A boss, with a backpack,
gives instructions to an employee at his start-up,

his voice full of the newness of command—
his jet-black hair like an Asian fan. I feel that
I'm not really here, like smoke from a cigarette

which has long since burnt out—the sun
as the only semblance of light we have for now.
A woman asks a man about the house in which

he lives, a mansion cut up into apartments,
of which he has one, the upper corner of a
dark gray stone building. She arrived at the most

interesting part of her conversation, the beautiful
historic section back in her hometown of East
Grand Rapids: pretty Victorians as far as

painted sky. My only regret, that I didn't share
the same conversation—my eyes not
as wide on this day far from Kalamazoo.

Wise and Innocent

Jesus said to his disciples: You know that in the world
rulers lord it over their subjects and make their power felt.
This is not to happen to you. No, anyone who wants to be
great among you must be your servant.

MARK 10:42–45

Her eyes are the smoking firmament, her
smile the unaccounted for bliss of Christmas:
the "no" within me that says this cannot

exist. Both teacher and student, she strides
off with her briefcase to teach class—tanned
as the slivers of her hair glistening:

light from light in the only way I know.
Yellow buildings surround "the cut" like Indians
in some hackneyed refilming of *Custer's Last*

Stand. Students order from a bank of trailers along
the only roadside on campus from which they can
buy lunch. Indian food changes hands

as if curry provided a currency of loss and redemption,
as if Margaret Morrison Hall had not yet become a school
for girls. Its striated pillars, the most beautiful

on campus. No one will tear it down, no history
covered over as if the blinking of our eyes mimic
the length of human memory. She greets me as she

walks to and from daily meetings, my chutney before
me in Styrofoam subtlety before the breeze: her next
words like the last, and eyes that leave me untethered.

The Distance from Here to There

Children dig in their sandbox like backhoes
before their dump trucks, in their canary
yellow peaceful arrays, black wheels knobby

as sneakers plow their way through like
the ladybug over my keyboard. The past
and present ally themselves as silicates,

crystalline before November sun, the hoods
of children drooping somberly, the slant
of light leaning serenely over freeze-dried

leaves: the most golden brown imaginable,
like buttered skins upon their tins. Beneath
their hoods are the faces of determined

workers, as their monitors watch over with
stork-like proclivity—an astronomer plotting
the parallax between red plastic hoe and

yellow metallic vehicle, a poet well aware
of the living circle of lives amidst the
glowing circles glinting off of silicates.

And I am at the fence, where a leaf has been
caught in the diamond mesh—right angles of
steel bearing childrens' approximations of stars.

Brussels Sprouts

Its image spreads out over the canvas
like a spine turned upside down, the green
pelvis freely splayed at the top of the page—

women hunting for their favorites
among multitudinous herbs, their skirts
cut just above the knee: just enough

to display a sense of freedom, more
than any Victorian could have dreamed
of. Outside, Sky stands dressed in its best

blues after sunset—muscular clouds
dipped in soot, unaccompanied desire
beneath their white tops: almost aimless.

The day has long since striven past
on gaudy legs reaching upward forever,
Saint Brigid even here in Pittsburgh

making her way through the verdant
cut of this campus. The green of
brussels sprouts did not come through

on the invitations as it does in the original,
art from art losing something in translation,
from gray to green: a longing for something real.

Crystalline

Young Canadian geese amass for the long
flight south, great breezes blowing them
into a zero alignment instead of a V,

their brownish-gray bodies upon gray sky,
leaves vaguely trailing behind. Pigeons
pick fervently at the seeds of trees as

they too blow in the November breeze,
the threat of snow hanging like the best
melodramatic plot twist, the coats of college

students making them seem uncharacteristically
young like too big children in their parkas,
the lack of time showing on bare hands

that either couldn't find mittens in time or
were never given the chance to go shopping.
In the air, snow hangs crystalline on pillows

of wind—their tiny whiteness as infant flakes
out playing before the parents would come
to rescue them from the real cold: the necks

of more experienced geese pointing south
like individual arrows in their collective V,
lost to all except the odd spectator and Heaven.

All Saints' Day

Black light filters over white sheets the
morning after a Halloween party, students
still somnolent after nightlong cheers for

more beer, that violet like visible silence
hanging in November winds, even the once
white curtains miming their filmy chorus

to the world. No one could have stopped
that cacophony, that nighttime brigade of
ghosts now laid to rest. Sky touches

Earth in times like these, Saint Brigid
bearing her heather in the only color she
now knows—violet upon violet before

the gaudy calliope of the mind. On campus,
plans already arise for the next big shindig,
their words more fervent than before,

designs to rival Sky and all that spills from
east to west. What could we know of it?
Somber is the sound the heart makes,

as we know of those who are alone,
but what of the sound the heart makes
when the world is filled with people like us?

All Souls' Day

for the film Mulholland Drive
(David Lynch, 2001)

The moon is full on Halloween for the first time
in forty-six years: bright yellow
of impressionable kitchens from commercials

in the sixties. These patrons have little feet,
slender souls going from door to door, demons
and angels wrapped in their respective stories

of the individual talent. On screen, another film
about a blonde who knows too much and
too little—a sparse audience and myself

caught in something like rapture with her
twiggy soprano honesty. Lithe to changing
wind, the moon twists in the November night

long after children have divvied up hard-
earned wages from black and orange bags.
Ours is a world of endless make-believe,

leaves masquerading even as the dark
splotches of eyes gone to rest in the grave
or the most somber chocolate chips

in ice cream after a break-up. The waning
moon will shine brightest on All Souls' Day,
the biggest contender on this night for our love.

Lessons in Nostalgia

A slender man walks with his little girl,
arm in arm along the trail taking in
trees and newfound individuals passing

by: every one a lesson in humanity—
a woman in her black jumper
and white blouse as one portion

of a backgammon board, another in her
pink blouse and purple skirt like an Easter
egg delicately moving in the most improbable

of circumstances. An aimless man watches
it all wondering which relationships seem
most difficult: those with sisters, wives,

or daughters? Sky has nothing left but the
last huffing before winter. Saint Brigid
wanders alone in the thin places

of contentment. An automobile passes in
its opal and white translucence as if harkening
back to the days of pure chrome and steel.

He views the women walking by in his nostalgia
for some simple life, faces of all varieties hovering
past on figures which might be love or happenstance.

Enigmatic

Trees nearly denuded, sky a platinum blue,
there is complete silence in the too white
clouds hovering over like campers before

the insects which they've collected. Leaves
tumble over the ground like kites, their brown
skins an agreement on the necessary color

of contentment and contemplation. The
chewed out pomegranates of installation
art hang from strings upon an oak tree, many

of its leaves still present, photographs tied around
the trunk and splattered with red as if the tree
had been bleeding out in its captivity. Past lives

receive endless visits by the symbols of today,
the hoary image of a woman seemingly kissing
a man splotched in pomegranate juice like a

new kind of sinning when no woman has ever
kissed a man just like that—or so I was told
by another onlooker. When looking carefully,

a particular kind of love seems rare just because it represents
the particular. Everyone wants the apple to remain that
symbol when others abound about our truer selves.

Apogee

Jet exhaust streams the sky; smoke rises
from cigarettes just outside of passage-
ways; the few remaining steel mills

pour smoke into the air in the only
refuge of microscopic particles. Indoors,
nothing remains but domesticity.

Only poems in my thirty-second year
could cure that peculiar silence where
the sound of children is like the sound

that smoke makes when clinging to
curtains. I see no footprints
leading back to my youth like

aphorisms on wooden placards,
the glistening plate an apogee
to the heart. In a time when

the lack of footsteps make up a speech
all their own, the "no" and "yes"
ambivalently the same, movies

can make it all seem like a wish for
more wishes in the filmy residue
of what the heart believes it wants.

Triptych

I

A woman selects the oldest piece of fruit
in the produce isle, places it firmly in her
basket, moves as if assisted by thunder,

as if Gabriel descended. A man
chooses a vest because he believes
that no one else will desire its

crosshatch cotton suppleness, because
he will presumably remain alone in this
thin place of existence. A child tunes

in to a comedy on the life of a struggling
artist instead of another show about
physicians, feeling that we know enough

about the lives of television doctors already.
Even in this universe, we know those who
endure solitude—those who might not comprehend

the necessity of another martyr to sustain some
all but lost cause. For all that has passed us by,
for every cloud lined with the silk of our dreams,

there are others where that lining is made of
wire mesh, only the thin places of our desire
enduring where all of us are alone together.

II

Perfect lawns stand like Easter basket
grass, plastic perfection, the too green
glistening surprisingly not too much

to take in. Molecules of lipstick move,
as if all on their own, as a woman
speaks from behind that veil of red—

the universe twinned in two velvet pieces
of rope. A cigarette hits wet pavement
in the "whep" signifying a much larger

butt, the shiny bricks made even more
electroplate as November rain pours,
the droplets like cold metal falling.

All this could belong to no one in
particular, martyrs who know little
about love, the whole of creation

going to waste in paintings and poems
as if Saint Brigid does not watch over us.
Where would that leave the handmaidens

of circumstance, the bridegrooms of
desire, the last among us who possibly
hear the only call that might matter?

III

My ghostly apparition in his blue-collar
life, working for Chrysler, is married,
is not as good a dresser, yet still has

kids who admire his gray and blue
plaid work shirt. No flowers
grow in his garden, only grass

bordered by wire mesh knee-high fences,
the job taking all of his time, the tub
packed with the dirt of that time.

Blessings seem hard to come by when
we need them most, as blessings resemble
the lives of fairies—lithe and ambivalent

and as resistant to focus as the gnat flitting
before binoculars. My prayers have not
been humble, nor have they been anything

like blue-collar dreams of getting over
amidst the most dire of financial circumstances.
There are white horses who could not

star in my dreams. There are Cadillacs that
are not quite classic enough. And when my woman
says "yes," it would make all of that seem like waste.

Acknowledgments

These poems also appear in print in the following publications, sometimes in alternate versions.

PERIODICALS

ABZ, "Fretwork"

Christianity and Literature, "Voices' End"

Cimarron Review, "Eight Modes toward Desire"

Crab Orchard Review, "Enigmatic"

Gloss, "The Memory of Light"

The Missouri Review, "Intercession to Saint Brigid," "Mist and Fog," and "Song of Earth and Sky"

Pittsburgh Post-Gazette, "The Distance from Here to There"

ANTHOLOGIES

The Autumn House Anthology of American Poems and Prayers, "Thin Places"

Collections, Fetishes, and Obsessions, "The Memory of Light"